BROADWAY VOCAL SELECTIONS

Sweet Charity
the musical comedy

©1986 Columbia Pictures Publications
15800 N.W. 48th Avenue, Miami, Florida 33014
Layout: Leyla Arner/Editor: David C. Olsen
Production: Frank J. Hackinson and Eric Colodne

CY COLEMAN

(Composer) came to music early, having performed at the piano in Steinway, Town and Carnegie halls between the ages of six and nine. Many of his songs have become standards, including "Witchcraft," "Hey Look Me Over," "Big Spender," "The Best Is Yet to Come," and "If My Friends Could See Me Now." He was honored at a star-studded tribute at Avery Fisher Hall and is one of the most versatile and influential craftsmen in the music industry. For the musical sensation *Barnum* he won 1980 Tony nominations as both composer and co-producer as well as duo 1981 Grammy nominations for the best original cast album. He won a Tony for his previous Broadway musical, *On the Twentieth Century,* which also toured the U.S. and played London. *I Love My Wife,* which opened the year before, also toured the U.S. with Tom and Dick Smothers. His other Broadway shows include *Little Me, Wildcat* and *Seesaw.* He won two Emmys for writing Shirley MacLaine's TV special "If They Could See Me Now," and another for her "Gypsy in My Soul," which he co-authored and co-produced. He has scored such films as *Father Goose, Power, Garbo Talks* and *Sweet Charity,* for which he won an Oscar nomination. He has also been honored with twelve Grammy nominations, seven Tony nominations and six Emmy nominations and has received a Tony, three Emmys, and two Drama Desk awards, among others. He is President of Notable Music Co., Inc. and serves on the Board of Directors of ASCAP.

DOROTHY FIELDS

(Lyrics). The name of Dorothy Fields on a PLAYBILL enlivened many a theatre season. Daughter of Lew Fields—of Webber and Fields vaudeville fame—Dorothy Fields, with her late brother Herbert, wrote the book of *Let's Face It* starring Danny Kaye, *Something for the Boys* starring Ethel Merman, and *Mexican Hayride,*, all having music and lyrics by Cole Porter; *Up in Central Park* with Sigmund Romberg; *Annie Get Your Gun,* for Ethel Merman, with music and lyrics by Irving Berlin and *By the Beautiful Sea* and *A Tree Grows in Brooklyn,* both starring Shirley Booth, with Arthur Schwartz. Miss Fields' first interest in the theatre was as a song-writer and among the great contemporary composers with whom she collaborated were Fritz Kreisler, Harold Arlen, Morton Gould, Jimmy McHugh, Oscar Levant, J. Fred Coots, Harry Warren and Jerome Kern. Some of the popular song hits to bear the Dorothy Fields name are "I Can't Give You Anything But Love," "Sunny Side of the Street," "I Won't Dance," "A Fine Romance," "I Feel a Song Coming On," "Lovely to Look At," "I'll Buy You a Star," "Pick Yourself Up," "Remind Me" and the Oscar Award-winning "The Way You Look Tonight," with music by Jerome Kern. Miss Fields penned the book and wrote the lyrics for *Redhead,* starring Gwen Verdon, with music by Albert Hague, which won six Tony Awards. Miss Fields died in 1974.

DEBBIE ALLEN (Charity), a graduate of Howard University, a student of Tapiana S. Semenova, Richard Thomas, George Faison, Jo Jo Smith and Uta Hagan, made her Broadway debut in the chorus of *Purlie* and went on to star in Tony Award-winning *Raisin,* which brought her instant recognition; *Ain't Misbehavin'*; and the 1979 production of *West Side Story* as Anita, for which she received a Tony Award nomination and Drama Desk Award. Her theatrical credits include Adelaide in the national company of *Guys and Dolls, Tijean and His Brothers* at the New York Shakespeare Festival, *Alice at the Palace* with Meryl Streep and Off-Broadway in the New Federal Theatre's production of *Anna Lucasta.* Debbie is adored by a loyal international television audience as the dance teacher, Lydia Grant, on "Fame," the successful syndicated series now in its sixth season. She is also well respected by the film industry as "Fame's" choreographer-director and co-producer. She has won two Emmys for her choreography on "Fame" and a Golden Globe Award as Best Actress in a Television Series. She also starred, choreographed, directed and produced the *Fame* stage show which toured throughout Europe in 1983 to SRO crowds. Debbie has made many guest appearances on television series and specials: NBC's "3 Girls 3," "Roots: The Next Generation" as Alex Haley's wife, the award winning special "Ben Vereen ... His Roots," David Gerber's "The Women of San Quentin," "The Academy Awards," "The Grammy Awards," Alexander Cohen's "Parade of Stars," "Motown's Return to the Apollo," "The Martin Luther King Birthday Celebration" and "Dancing in the Wings," a one-hour special for L.B.S. Communications which she co-executive produced, co-wrote, choreographed and starred. Debbie returns to feature films this year in Richard Pryor's highly anticipated semi-autobiographical film, *Jo Jo Dancer, Your Life is Calling.* Her other films included Milos Forman's *Ragtime* and *The Fish That Saved Pittsburgh.* Away from the bright lights, Debbie has two favorite roles— wife of NBA All-Star guard Norman Nixon and mother to their baby daughter, Vivian Nichole.

TIME AND PLACE
NEW YORK — MID 1960s
SYNOPSIS OF SCENES AND MUSICAL NUMBERS
ACT I
PROLOGUE— CHARITY'S THEME

Scene 1. THE PARK
You Should See Yourself .... Debbie Allen, David Warren Gibson
The Rescue .... The Passers-by

Scene 2. HOSTESS ROOM

Scene 3. FAN-DANGO BALLROOM
Big Spender .... Bebe Neuwirth, Allison Williams and
the Fan-Dango Girls

Scene 4. NEW YORK STREET

Scene 5. POMPEII CLUB
Rich Man's Frug .... Dana Moore, Kelly Patterson,
Adrian Rosario—The Patrons

Scene 6. VITTORIO VIDAL'S APARTMENT
If My Friends Could See Me Now .... Debbie Allen
Too Many Tomorrows .... Mark Jacoby

Scene 7. HOSTESS ROOM
There's Gotta Be Something Better Than This .... Debbie Allen,
Bebe Neuwrith, Allison Williams

Scene 8. 92nd STREET "Y"
I'm The Bravest Individual .... Debbie Allen, Michael Rupert

ACT II

Scene 1. 92nd STREET "Y"

Scene 2. RHYTHM OF LIFE CHURCH
Rhythm Of Life .... Irving Allen Lee, Tanis Michaels,
Stanley Wesley Perryman and Worshippers

Scene 3. GOING CROSS-TOWN

Scene 4. CHARITY'S APARTMENT
Baby Dream Your Dream .... Bebe Neuwirth and Allison Williams

Scene 5. CONEY ISLAND
Sweet Charity .... Michael Rupert

Scene 6. FAN-DANGO BALLROOM

Scene 7. TIMES SQUARE
Where Am I Going .... Debbie Allen

Scene 8. BARNEY'S CHILE HACIENDA

Scene 9. *I'm A Brass Band* .... Debbie Allen and her Brass Band

Scene 10. FAN-DANGO BALLROOM
I Love To Cry At Weddings .... Lee Wilkof, Tom Wierney,
Bebe Neuwirth, Allison Williams, Girls and Patrons

Scene 11. THE PARK

From The Musical Comedy "SWEET CHARITY"

CHARITY'S THEME

Music by
CY COLEMAN

Lyric by
DOROTHY FIELDS

Sweet Charity Theme - 2 - 1

7

Sweet Charity Theme - 2 - 2

From The Musical Comedy "SWEET CHARITY"

YOU SHOULD SEE YOURSELF

Music by
CY COLEMAN

Lyric by
DOROTHY FIELDS

You Should See Yourself - 4 - 1

10

You Should See Yourself - 4 - 3

From The Musical Comedy "SWEET CHARITY"

BIG SPENDER

Music by
CY COLEMAN

Lyric by
DOROTHY FIELDS

Big Spender - 3 - 1

good time.___ Let me show you a good time.___ The min-ute you

Hey, Big Spend-er!___ Hey, Big Spend-er!___

Spend_____ a lit-tle time_ with me, Spend a lit-tle time_ with

me, Spend a lit-tle time_ with me._____

D. S. al Coda

Coda

From The Musical Comedy "SWEET CHARITY"

IF MY FRIENDS COULD SEE ME NOW!

Music by
CY COLEMAN

Lyric by
DOROTHY FIELDS

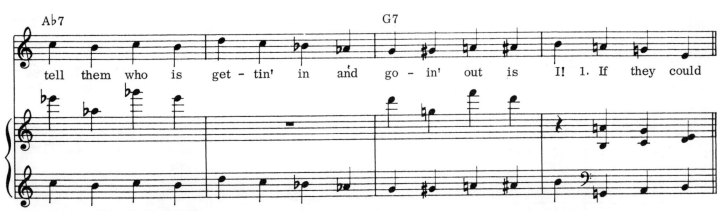

If My Friends Could See Me Now! - 3 - 1

16

If My Friends Could See Me Now! - 3 - 2

If My Friends Could See Me Now! - 3 - 3

From The Musical Comedy "SWEET CHARITY"

TOO MANY TOMORROWS

Music by
CY COLEMAN

Lyric by
DOROTHY FIELDS

Too Many Tomorrows - 2 - 1

Too Many Tomorrows - 2 - 2

From The Musical Comedy "SWEET CHARITY"

THERE'S GOTTA BE SOMETHING BETTER THAN THIS

Music by
CY COLEMAN

Lyric by
DOROTHY FIELDS

There's Gotta Be Something Better Than This - 4 - 1

get up,   I'm gon - na   get out,   I'm gon - na   get up,   get out and   {do it!
                                                                                   {learn it!

Tambourine

1.   F   2.   C   C7

There's got-ta be   No more

Fmaj7   F6   E7   Am7   D7   Eb7   D7

grip - ing,_____   I have   had   it,_____   No more   groan - ing,

There's Gotta Be Something Better Than This - 4 - 2

There's Gotta Be Something Better Than This - 4 - 3

There's Gotta Be Something Better Than This - 4 - 4

From The Musical Comedy "SWEET CHARITY"

I'M THE BRAVEST INDIVIDUAL

Music by
CY COLEMAN

Lyric by
DOROTHY FIELDS

I'm The Bravest Individual - 5 - 1

I'm the brav-est in-di-vid-u-al I have ev-er met."

Vamp under dialogue

Oscar:

Why is it

sud-den-ly I can't swal-low?— Can't seem to fo-cus an eye.— Right now my

sto-mach's an emp-ty hol-low;— I think I'm go-ing to die. Just

Charity:

28

From The Musical Comedy "SWEET CHARITY"

THE RHYTHM OF LIFE

Music by
CY COLEMAN

Lyric by
DOROTHY FIELDS

Dad-dy start-ed out in San Fran-cis-co, toot-in' on a trum-pet loud and mean,

Sud-den-ly a voice said, "Go forth, Dad-dy, spread the pic-ture on a

wid-er screen." And the voice said, "Broth-er, there's a mil-lion pi-geons

The Rhythm Of Life - 8 - 1

From The Musical Comedy "SWEET CHARITY"

BABY DREAM YOUR DREAM

Music by
CY COLEMAN

Lyric by
DOROTHY FIELDS

Baby Dream Your Dream - 3 - 1

From The Musical Comedy "SWEET CHARITY"

SWEET CHARITY

Music by
CY COLEMAN

Lyric by
DOROTHY FIELDS

Sweet Charity - 3 - 1

44

From The Musical Comedy "SWEET CHARITY"

WHERE AM I GOING?

Music by
CY COLEMAN

Lyric by
DOROTHY FIELDS

Where Am I Going? - 4 - 1

Copyright © 1965 by Dorothy Fields and Cy Coleman
All rights throughout the world controlled by NOTABLE MUSIC CO., INC., New York, NY 10019
In Co-publication with LIDA ENTERPRISES, INC.
International Copyright Secured   Made In U.S.A.   All Rights Reserved

From The Musical Comedy "SWEET CHARITY"

I'M A BRASS BAND

Music by
CY COLEMAN

Lyric by
DOROTHY FIELDS

I'm A Brass Band - 3 - 1

I'm A Brass Band - 3 - 2

From The Musical Comedy "SWEET CHARITY"

I LOVE TO CRY AT WEDDINGS

Music by
CY COLEMAN

Lyric by
DOROTHY FIELDS

March tempo

I Love To Cry At Wed-dings, how I Love To Cry At Wed-dings, I walk in-to a chap-el and get hap-pi-ly hys-ter-i-cal, The ush-ers and at-tend-ants, the fam-i-ly de-pen-dents, I see them and I start to sniff, have you an ex-tra

I Love To Cry At Weddings - 2 - 1

I Love To Cry At Weddings - 2 - 2

From The Musical Comedy "SWEET CHARITY"

CHARITY'S THEME

Music by CY COLEMAN
Lyric by DOROTHY FIELDS

From The Musical Comedy "SWEET CHARITY"

YOU SHOULD SEE YOURSELF

Music by CY COLEMAN
Lyric by DOROTHY FIELDS

From The Musical Comedy "SWEET CHARITY"

BIG SPENDER

Music by CY COLEMAN
Lyric by DOROTHY FIELDS

From The Musical Comedy "SWEET CHARITY"

IF MY FRIENDS COULD SEE ME NOW!

Music by CY COLEMAN
Lyric by DOROTHY FIELDS

Verse 2:
If they could see me now, my little dusty group,
Traipsin' 'round this million dollar chicken coop.
I'd hear those thrift shop cats say: "Brother, get her!
Draped on a bedspread made from three kinds of fur."
All I can say is, "Wow! Wait till the riff and raff
See just exactly how he signed this autograph."
What a buildup! Holy cow! They'd never believe it,
If my friends could see me now.

Verse 3:
If they could see me now, alone with Mister V.,
Who's waitin' on me like he was a maitre d'.
I hear my buddies saying: "Crazy, what gives?
Tonight she's living like the other half lives."
To think the highest brow, which I must say is he
Should pick the lowest brow, which there's no doubt is me.
What a step up! Holy cow! They'd never believe it,
If my friends could see me now.

From The Musical Comedy "SWEET CHARITY"

TOO MANY TOMORROWS

Music by CY COLEMAN
Lyric by DOROTHY FIELDS

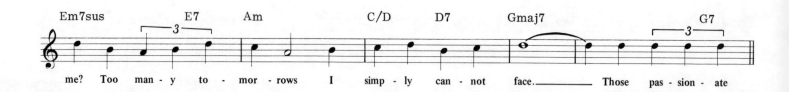

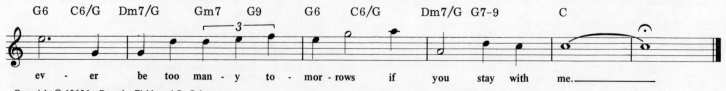

From The Musical Comedy "SWEET CHARITY"

THERE'S GOTTA BE SOMETHING BETTER THAN THIS

Music by CY COLEMAN
Lyric by DOROTHY FIELDS

From The Musical Comedy "SWEET CHARITY"

I'M THE BRAVEST INDIVIDUAL

Music by CY COLEMAN
Lyric by DOROTHY FIELDS

From The Musical Comedy "SWEET CHARITY"

BABY DREAM YOUR DREAM

Music by CY COLEMAN
Lyric by DOROTHY FIELDS

Moderate Swing

1. Ba - by, dream your dream.___ Close your eyes and try___ it.
2. Dream we sign the lease,___ leave a small de - pos - it;
3. Ev - 'ry Sat - ur - day,___ we'll spend all our mon - ey.

Dream of fur - ni - ture;___ dream that I can buy___ it. That fan - cy
Three - and - one - half rooms___ with a walk - in clos - et. We'll ask the
Join the P. T. A.;___ they will love you, hon - ey. Life will be

bed you prayed___ for, not on - ly bought, but paid___ for.
lo - cal jet___ set

to dine on our din-ette___ set.

Right a - cross the street,___ there's a friend - ly bank.___ You make a

friend - ly loan,___ and the bank says, "Thank___ you."

fro - zen peach - es and

cream. Ba - by, dream your dream.___

From The Musical Comedy "SWEET CHARITY"

THE RHYTHM OF LIFE

Music by CY COLEMAN
Lyric by DOROTHY FIELDS

From The Musical Comedy "SWEET CHARITY"

SWEET CHARITY

Music by CY COLEMAN
Lyric by DOROTHY FIELDS

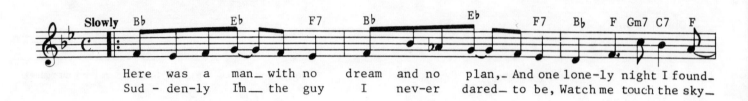

Here was a man_ with no dream and no plan,_ And one lone-ly night I found_
Sud-den-ly I'm_ the guy I nev-er dared_ to be, Watch me touch the sky_

_ Sweet Char-i-ty. You make life fun_ for me, oh, what it's done_ for me,
_ quite eas-i-ly.

Hav-ing you a-round,_ Sweet Char-i-ty. Warm words I've nev-er said_ late-ly

Pop off the top of my head,_ it's in-cred-i-ble._ So if you are free

_ Sweet Char-i-ty, Please be-long_ to me, Sweet Char-i-ty, Please be-long-to me,

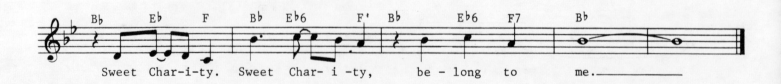

Sweet Char-i-ty. Sweet Char-i-ty, be-long to me._

From The Musical Comedy "SWEET CHARITY"

WHERE AM I GOING?

Music by CY COLEMAN
Lyric by DOROTHY FIELDS

From The Musical Comedy "SWEET CHARITY"

I'M A BRASS BAND

Music by CY COLEMAN
Lyric by DOROTHY FIELDS

From The Musical Comedy "SWEET CHARITY"

I LOVE TO CRY AT WEDDINGS

Music by CY COLEMAN
Lyric by DOROTHY FIELDS

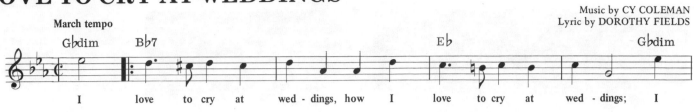

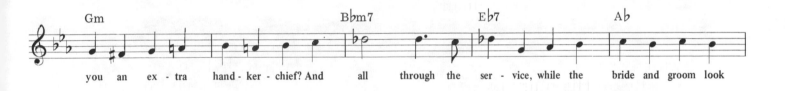

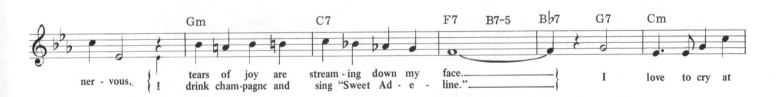

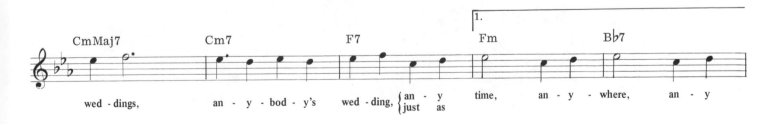

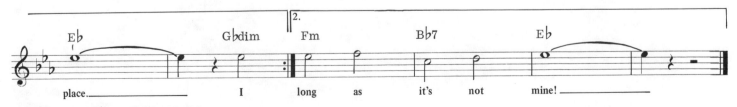